THEY chose to be GREAT

THEY chose to be GREAT

Inspiring Stories of Service by
Massachusetts Foster Youth

Edited By Milton and Debbie Drake

They Chose to be Great:
Inspiring Stories of Service by Massachusetts Foster Youth

Cover design: Jennifer Maugel
Interior design: Thais Gloor

This book is dedicated to the 23 young heroes
you will meet in the following pages,
who have chosen to live a life of significance
by service to others.

Acknowledgements

We would like to say thank you to:

Michelle Banks—Program Supervisor for Adolescent Support Services for the MA Department of Children and Families, whose love and vision for foster youth has been a constant inspiration and encouragement behind their growth and ongoing development.

Jeanie Shaw—author, friend, and invaluable resource for bringing the book to print.

The MLK Scholarship Committee—Kim Farmer, Helen Devlin, Ilona Sewell, Kristen Colon, and Susan Dollar. You have all spent countless hours to make an idea a reality.

Linda Wilkinson—Debbie's sister, confidant and friend, who lightly corrected each winning essay without altering the spirit or message of the writer.

Contents

Part Five: They Chose to Become Leaders by
          Standing up for Others

Part Six: Next Steps in Living a Life of Significance

Foreword

As a Social Worker in the field of child welfare, I see how difficult life and development can be for adolescents who live in a world dictated by circumstances far beyond their personal control. Yet, I also see resilience emerge in these young people very early in life as they have faced uncertainty and met challenges at a deeper and more complex level than most of their peers and even the adults in their lives.

One might consider that as adolescents recover from the experience of trauma and continue to search for their own identity, and pursue their own goals in circumstances that involve family crisis, that other matters may limit the interest in or availability for service to others. In my experience though it has been quite the opposite. The will and drive to help others among the DCF adolescent population is prevalent. Many of them report leading school fundraisers, or mentoring younger children, holding office on school/community councils, or caring for younger foster siblings. Our own Adolescent Outreach Program nurtures our youth leaders to serve and helps them to become active on youth advisory boards, become trainers of new foster and adoptive parents, and support foster youth peers through groups and networking events. The interest and abilities these adolescents have in serving their communities and families is limitless.

Therefore, in 2010, when HOPE worldwide approached the DCF Kids Fund about inviting our foster youth to compete for college scholarships via an essay contest focused on service, I knew it was going to be something special.

The contest would ask our young people to read an excerpt of a speech made by Dr. Martin Luther King, Jr. known as the "Drum Major" speech. In it, Dr. King emphasizes the biblical concept of service; if they want to be first at something—be the first to serve, the first to stand up for justice.

While I was confident our youth were strong in their community service experiences, I wondered how they would be able to reflect on their service in the form of an essay and relate to Dr. King's message. It took one essay contest and one award ceremony for this question to be answered. Yes! They fully grasped the message of the drum major speech. Yes! They serve their communities at every level in creative, thoughtful, and entrepreneurial fashions. Yes! Not only can they write about it, they can articulate how they came to value the opportunity to serve and explain how they are working to overcome the trauma they have experienced.

The youth who share their experiences in these essays come from every corner of the globe and have experienced the spectrum of the human condition. They have witnessed and/or experienced extreme conflict but also true kindness. They understand what is needed to help an individual or family or community in crisis, whether that is sharing a talent in fundraisers, donating time through tutoring or counseling, helping to raise awareness in systems and communities, and in doing so serving all generations and levels of need.

One common theme throughout the essays is the connection the youth have to their families and their culture. Regardless of what happened in their past, the youth see their backgrounds as a strength and often choose to serve those who share their culture and in addition share their struggle in a broader context. Another important theme across the essays is that in serving their communities these youth recognize that they are serving themselves. As they grow to be adults, they deeply understand how critical the role of a helper is, and how shame and stigma have no place in communities that truly want to thrive.

I believe Dr. King would consider these young men and women his partners in the quest for social justice. I would like to thank these young people and HOPE worldwide for allowing my colleagues and I to be part of such a worthy endeavor.

Michelle Banks, MSW, LCSW
Program Supervisor, Adolescent Support Services
Massachusetts Department of Children and Families

Introduction

Do you long for meaning in your life? Are you stuck in a rut? Are you invigorated by hope?

As you turn the next few pages you will be inspired and challenged by young men and women who could have easily given up, yet instead became beacons of hope. They have found meaning and adventure in their lives—and at tender young ages are driven by their hopes and dreams. These local heroes show us how "it" is done.

I've witnessed "it" within men and women living in homes atop a garbage heap. I've seen "it" in South African mothers with AIDS as they cared for their children. I've seen "it" in India when victims of leprosy came together as a caring village. And now I see "it" in the lives of teens and young adults, who as a result of various traumas, found themselves in foster care. Through opportunities provided by HOPE worldwide to work with the underserved throughout the world, "it" has moved me, convicted me, and changed me.

So just what is "it?"

"It" is that desire born within us, despite our circumstances or how we may be viewed, to make our lives count. "It" is a passion for life that has order and meaning. "It" is the passion to become what God created us to be—givers.

In this inspiring collection of essays, you will hear "it" through voices of young men and women who are overcoming seemingly insurmountable odds. They have learned, and are continually learning, the great paradox of God—it is in giving that we receive.

These young men and women have made a choice. A choice to move past the bricks of pain and mistrust that paved their paths. They uprooted those bricks and with them built a bridge of hope for others to cross—and in the process found "it." They have discovered joy and meaning through service.

They made a choice and took a chance. A chance to change the world and thus change themselves.

A chance to change themselves and thus change the world.

My grandson, Micah, recently had a conversation with my husband (his Papa) who suffers from a progressive neurological disease and can no longer walk. Micah assured his Papa that he prayed every day for him to get better. My husband explained to him that we don't always know or understand how God answers our prayers, but we can know that he cares, loves, and strengthens us as we rely on him for our journey. Micah then reassured Papa with the statement, "You know Papa, every day is a new chance."

Truer words could not be spoken. Every day is a new chance—a chance to serve, to love, and to make a difference in someone's life.

As I write this introduction from my kitchen chair, I observe a little sign I've placed on the windowsill. It is one of the few possessions I kept from my father after he passed— as it exemplifies his attitude toward life. An overcomer, he was a man of great integrity whose life blessed many others. The little sign simply reads, "Now tell me all the reasons it can be done."

The young men and women you will hear from in this book have adopted these attitudes. They defy the excuses that tell them "it" can't be done, and they believe that every day offers a new chance. Through raw and resilient benev-olence these young men and women are changing the world, one life at a time.

Dr. Milton and Debbie Drake, who edited this book, have been passionately serving around the world, as well as in their own Massachusetts "back yard," for many years as they practice the "it" factor. Dr. Drake (a well-respected and still practicing physician in his mid-seventies) along with his wife Debbie (a health educator), long to make a differ-ence in the lives they touch. They seek to let voices not often heard inspire us. Thus, they began a scholarship op-portunity for teens and young adults who are (or have been) in foster care. Each year these young men and women are given an opportunity to share (via essays) the impact service has had on their lives, and the way other service heroes, specifically Dr. Martin Luther King, Jr., inspire them. Their words were too inspiring to keep filed away. Thus, this book was born.

As you read the stories of these young adults, consider their obstacles as they follow their dreams. Let their voices inspire you to dig deeply into the resources of your heart— and to serve like never before. In so doing, you will find in-describable joy. It truly is more blessed to give than to receive.

Jeanie Shaw
Women's minister, author, and former
HOPE worldwide vice-president

PART ONE

They Chose to Overcome

"Everyone has the power for greatness,
not for fame but greatness,
because greatness is determined by service."[1]

1

Walking in Dr. King's Footprints

As a refugee from the Democratic Republic of Congo, which I left during the Civil War in 1999, I could speak few words in English, much less understand the American accent. However, about four years ago when I first came to the US after spending 9 years in a Refugee Camp in Zambia after leaving Congo, I realized that without the help of others I would not be able to accomplish any of my goals. I decided that I needed help to be able to catch up with other students who were already on the move. I found out about the ACE (African Community Education) program, which provides extra academic help besides school for immigrant and refugee students. Through the program, I experienced the spirit of serving others. This shaped and changed my ways of approaching and dealing with life obstacles, including schoolwork.

Throughout my junior and senior years of high school, I committed myself to helping others by giving back to my community. Besides going back to ACE where I volunteered helping other students who were facing the same academic difficulties as I did few a years before, I was also fully involved in my school academic and extra-curricular activities. I helped my school win the Varsity Soccer Championship for two consecutive years 2010-2011; I was a member of the Student Honor Society; and a member of the High School

Advisory Council during my junior and senior years at North High School in Worcester, Massachusetts. I am also the recipient of the ASOST (After School and Out of School Time) Achievement Award by the Massachusetts Afterschool Partnership.

My hard work and resilient spirit throughout my four years of high school paid off last year when I received an acceptance letter from Boston College where I am currently enrolled as a freshman student. During the summer school program at Boston College known as OTE (Option Through Education), I had the opportunity to do community service at a food bank for the less fortunate in Boston. This service gave me the opportunity not only to receive but also serve others. I always give thanks to the Almighty God who made it possible for me to be in this great nation. I am thankful for the ideas, philosophy, inspiration, and works of Dr. Martin Luther King. Right now at Boston College, I joined two student clubs, the FYI against racial discrimination, and the AHANA for African American, Hispanic and Asian Minority students.

Since I was a freshman in high school, I was captivated by the struggle of Dr. King and the Civil Rights Movement. It encouraged me to believe in the American Dream. I came to understand that without the non-violent struggle that Dr. King led about half a century ago for freedom and equality, someone like me would not have had the confidence to dream big and hope for a better and bright future. But, today I can say that the vision that Dr. Martin Luther King had for his country is being fulfilled in our time. His selfless character and his spirit of serving others have influenced my decision to serve others. I would say that I draw my strength and inspiration from the dream of love, peace, and service that Dr. King envisioned for America and the world, and I am committed to walk in his footprints as a good citizen by serving my community and country.

Issa A. Noel
2013 2nd Place Winner

2

Serving to Make the World Better

I believe that it does not take a genius to know that our world today is in turmoil. Depictions of oppressed individuals are aired on television daily. We see homeless people begging for help in the streets, parents losing their jobs, children going to bed on empty stomachs, and many other heartbreaking situations in our community and all over the world. Fortunately, a number of organizations have emerged and work hard to bring lasting solutions to victims. Due to these generous organizations, some individuals are being saved from the horrors of hunger, genocide, and many other forms of oppression. I too, was once a victim of genocide in the Congo, but because of non-profit organizations such as the United Nations High Commissioner for Refugees (UNHCR), and the Massachusetts department of Children and Families (DCF), I am no longer a victim. I am a survivor.

I cannot help but wonder, what about other victims? What is to happen to those not fortunate enough to receive the assistance with which I was blessed? Since the organizations that are working hard to help victims can only go so far, does this mean that those who were "unlucky" will be left to suffer? Questions like these are what fuel my drive to be an active member in my community and to aid in helping others find hope and peace.

My own experiences have forged an empathetic link between myself and those in need. This link has provided motivation to become involved in a number of volunteer and fundraising works in an attempt to promote a positive change in the world. For example, I am currently a member of the African Student Association (ASA) at Bridgewater State University. This organization serves to increase awareness of different issues going on in Africa such as wars emerging from cultural differences and also to educate young adults about how they can help solve major issues in Africa and other countries in need. Also, in Bridgewater State University's 2013 Relay for Life, I helped raise money to further research for a cancer cure.

Another cause close to my heart is World Vision, which serves to end hunger. Through the United Church of Christ (UCC) in Medfield and Maplewood Baptist Church in Malden I furthered their goal by participating in their 30 Hour Famine multiple times. In addition, I also participated in a half-marathon for the 2012 Boston's Run to Remember under Team World Vision and fundraised more money for World Vision. Taking part in these events only inspires me to give back more.

After each volunteer event, I feel a sense of accomplishment that is rooted in my first-hand experience of being a recipient. Since my life was forever changed by the generosity of others, I constantly see my story in the lives I am influencing through my work. This gives me a deeper appreciation of how fortunate I am to have come so far that I can now give back. Personal trials and tribulations have occurred but I can now appreciate the dedication that goes into these organizations and the difference each donation can make to a life.

One volunteer opportunity that solidified my understanding of the importance of giving back was the UCC's 2011 mission trip to the Pine Ridge Reservation in South Dakota. Working with Native Americans, I saw how their families were affected by poverty and found myself constantly reminded of my life in Africa. It allowed me to look past differences in location and ethnicity and draw comparisons to my life. I was humbled to see similarities in our experiences and, now, I always find myself offering a thankful prayer for my blessings.

I believe that everything happens for a reason, and I know that I was helped by many to become the man I am today. With the numerous blessings I have been given, it is now my mission to give back. My lifelong goal is to graduate college with the knowledge and skill set to go back to my homeland—Democratic Republic of Congo—and assist in helping those that are still oppressed by genocide. Until I achieve this goal, I intend to continue volunteering believing that one person CAN make a difference. After all, Martin Luther King Jr. himself said, "everybody can serve." Whether it is through organizations like the ASA, World Vision, or the UCC, I have found meaningful ways to channel my passion for service to the community just as they gave to me in my time of need.

Daniel Tabiale
2015 1st Place Winner

Life is a Journey

My memory of the past has greatly influenced me. I grew up in a country where not every parent could afford to pay for his children's school fees. I spent three full years without attending school because my siblings also needed to learn how to read and write. My parents and I experienced so many dilemmas that have now been transformed into a story of success. The only hope to get out of our difficult circumstances was to come to the United States of America. Coming from Africa to the United States has taught me a lot over the years. I came from a poor refugee family in the Democratic Republic of Congo. I lived and struggled with my parents as refugees in Uganda for years before being given the opportunity to resettle in the United States, which has proven to be a great land of freedom for us to start our lives over again.

Since I was young, my dream was always to help other people. Learning English as a second language became very helpful in my life. It gave me an opportunity to become a role model among my peers in helping them with their school homework and helping them feel at home when they arrived in the United States for the first time. I also helped them to join school activities such as clubs and sports, and encouraged them to do their work daily. If it had not been for the help that I received when I came to the United States,

I don't believe I would be a member of the National Honor Society today. As Martin Luther King, Jr. said, "The function of education is to teach one to think intensively and think critically. Intelligence plus character—that is the goal of true education."

To give back to my community and the people who helped me, I volunteer in local community activities such as the Lowell Public Library. I also support the International Institute of Lowell to resettle new families who are integrating into their new life in America. I have contributed my time at public events such as the Lowell Folk Festival. This has helped me improve my public speaking skills and has given me more confidence to speak in front of my peers.

Through the experiences I have gained, I am planning to help whoever is in need of school fees, food, and shelter. Because the help that I received is a blessing that I will never forget, I am willing to help others so that they can accomplish their dreams. Martin Luther King, Jr. said "I have a dream that my four little children will one day live in a nation where they will not be judged by the color of their skin, but by the content of their character." I, too, have a dream that one day I will open up a school to help people who need to continue with their studies.

Clarice Rwakabuba
2015 3rd Place Winner

Serving

Serving brings nothing but purity and a blessing to your wounded heart. Whatever you are going through in your life, there is always someone else that has it worse than you. That is why it is important for individuals to always be open to serving others less fortunate than themselves. Throughout history, great men have appeared from Martin Luther King to Gandhi, whose purpose was not glory and wealth but service. And because these selfless people served, they brought great change that affected millions of lives.

When I first became a foster child I wanted to give up, because not only was I new to America, but I was also abandoned by my father. I had nobody but a sister. However, getting involved and serving others completely saved my life. In school, I wanted to be the best that I could be. I was involved in so many different extracurricular activities. One in particular was at Somerville High School, where I volunteered to speak to elementary kids so that I could teach them how to better prepare for High School. These kids were very excited to get a glimpse into high school life, and it made them eager to excel in school so they could further their education. Seeing their eagerness showed me that helping others in the smallest ways has a big impact. From then on, I was determined to keep serving.

Another volunteer service I joined was Teen Empowerment in Somerville which helps youth going through difficult times in their life. While I was listening to their stories, I learned a lesson that I will never forget. Everyone has a story to tell and one story is not better than the other. The best thing a person can do is to be there; you never know what that could mean.

One memorable volunteering service I was part of was at Somerville Hospital as an assistant for anyone that needed my service. I helped elders get their food and manage their medication. I also typed and mailed papers out for some of the therapists that worked there. I fell in love with it and helping others became an addiction that kept me going in life towards a future career path in nursing.

In addition, I volunteered at a Court Yard Nursing Home where I cared for the elders. At first, it was difficult because a lot of them were scared to die and I didn't know what I was going to do to help ease their minds. I helped feed them, administered their medication, bathed them, and listened to their wonderful life stories. Doing this service for them showed me what humanity really means. Also, I could see hope in their eyes again, when they saw the care I was providing for them, even if it meant just having someone to talk to.

Lastly, I volunteered for the Special Olympics for Somerville High School. It was for any children in Somerville that had a mental disability. The point was to spend time with them and make their day more enjoyable. While I was working with them I noticed how much happier and hopeful they were. They go through so much pain and struggle in their life but when you look into their eyes, they're filled with light. Instead of making their day, they made mine. They made me appreciate life much more.

In conclusion, serving others doesn't just mean doing things for others; it's much bigger than that. It has to come from the heart, otherwise you'll miss the whole point. When you do it from the heart, you will get a true blessing. All the anger, fear, abandonment and hatred you have will be erased. That one smile you put on someone else's face and the hope you see in their eyes is greater than life itself.

Himonot Mulugeta
2014 1st place winner

Service as a Path to Happiness

Life in a refugee camp is not easy. When I was thirteen years old, my family was forced to flee to Uganda for safety because of the war in the Democratic Republic of Congo, my country of origin. Living in a refugee camp for a year was not easy. There was a lot of disease because of the over crowded population. In addition, the sleeping conditions were not good because of the cramped quarters. Even after moving out of the refugee camp, we lived a life as persecuted refugees in which we felt afraid of the people living around us.

After coming to the United States in 2009, I thought that my life would change. I thought that once all my material needs were met I would be happy. But I have come to learn that one cannot find joy and happiness in possessions. This became clear to me one day when the pastor at church quoted a Bible scripture from the book of Acts 20:35, in which Jesus told his disciples, "There is more happiness in giving than there is in receiving." After hearing this scripture, I started serving others both in the community in the refugee camp in Uganda, and then later in the United States. This eventually included the volunteering I did with Habitat for Humanity. In addition, when I started earning money at my part-time job in the United States I sent some of my money to friends who were still in the camps in Uganda.

Serving the people in the community has made me forget most of the horrible things I experienced while fleeing to Uganda from the Democratic Republic of the Congo. One of the things that I try to forget is the loss of my grandmother and my twin sister who went missing during our escape. These were the two people closest to me. I have come to learn that I am able to endure the pain of not having them in my life through helping those in need and knowing that I am making a difference in someone's life. In addition, through helping other people I have come to forget the pain of hunger and the feeling of insecurity in my community. Putting a smile on someone's face warms my heart and helps me forget that I have ever lived in a refugee camp.

The joy I feel from serving others has led me to consider pursuing a career in the medical field. I hope that one day I am able to help improve the health conditions in refugee camps. I am certain that it is not money or material things that brings happiness, but one's service to those in need that is the key to a happy life.

Bahati Mweze
2014 3rd place winner

Bringing Equality and Peace to the World

My name is Amber Biswa. I'm from Nepal, and I was born and grew up in a Refugee Camp. My parents are from Bhutan, but it was not a safe place, so they had to leave Bhutan.

They spoke only Nepali, so they moved to Nepal in 1992 and they lived under a bridge for one year without getting any support. They were not educated because they did not have the opportunity to attend school in Bhutan. They did not believe that education would help them in their future, but they did believe in hard work. Although my grandfather and uncles lacked education, they were good tradesmen and made knives.

Martin Luther King Jr. was an African American who wanted to eliminate segregation and bring peace and equality to the nation. He worked for the Civil Rights Movement and brought Black and White people together. He sacrificed his life to stop discrimination. He strongly believed that we are all human beings and deserve to be treated equally. He didn't want anybody to be judged by their skin color; instead, he wanted people to be judged by their character and attitude. He received a Nobel Peace Prize in 1964 for bringing the Nation together. Thus, he inspired me to help people who don't have any rights and need help. Martin Luther King Jr. made a difference in this world by serving other people, and I am trying to serve other people like he did. When I was young I started to serve my family, because we didn't have enough food and shelter to live. When I was twelve years old, I would work from 7am to 6pm crushing stones and carrying 50 pound bags of stones to a job site to earn money for my family. I earned 220 rupees per day, which is equal to $2.50. That's how I learned to care about other people.

Growing up in a Refugee Camp taught me to help others. In Nepal, I served my school and peers by taking on additional responsibilities and teaching them to stay on the right track. Many students followed my lead and also served their friends and families as well as society.

I am continuing this philosophy here in America by tutoring 7th graders and my peers at high school. Helping my peers makes me feel good and at peace.

In my community in Nepal we needed a lot of support so I was able to help when we encountered problems. I volunteered every night to be a watch guard at the Refugee Camp to ensure other people's safety. I also volunteered at the YMCA in Nepal to help children. When I came to the United States I continued to help my society. In the winter, I volunteered to shovel the snow on my neighbor's driveway, and in the fall I raked leaves for older people in the community. And I enjoyed doing it!

I am looking forward to serving people my whole life. Serving other people has helped me to learn a lot of new things. It has allowed me to meet many people, and get to know their feelings. I have also learned how to be respectful and honest. The main thing I have learned is that you should never judge people by their looks; instead, you should get to know them and respect them for who they are. I plan to go to college because I want to become a doctor. When I become a doctor I want to work for the non-profit organization, Doctors without Borders.

I really like to help people because I am aware that many people struggle and don't have the means to afford health care for their families. Helping others makes you different, and also makes you smart. I really want to give back to as many people as I can. If you make people smile, the world will be a better place. There will be less violence and discrimination if people respect and help each other, and so I want to be a good example for everybody. God created everybody equally, so everybody should be treated equally, no matter who they are and where they are from. I want to bring peace to this world by serving others.

Amber Biswa
2016 2nd Place Winner

PART TWO

They Chose to Encourage

"I have decided to stick with love. Hate is too great a burden to bear."[2]

The Push of Encouragement

"The King will reply, 'Truly I tell you, whatever you did for one of the least of these brothers and sisters of mine, you did for me.'"- Matthew 25:40

As I have grown up and matured, I have come to realize the true importance and necessity of serving others. Before high school, I did most of my volunteer work at my church. My grandparents pastor a church in the inner city of Dorchester in Boston. At our church, helping people in the community is one of our main priorities. Since about the age of twelve, I have been involved in our Annual Christmas Gala, where we receive toys from Toys for Tots and distribute them to the members of the community.

Once I entered high school, my volunteer work increased. I joined my school Food Pantry that is known for serving the community of Taunton, and volunteered at our National Honors Society Toy Gift Shop. This gift shop allowed parents to come shop for Christmas presents at our make shift shop for free, enabling them to provide their children with toys to wake up to on Christmas morning. After volunteering in this program, I was so moved by the influence we made on people's lives, that I participated in it all four years of high school. The joy and relief seen in each parent's face after they had a bag full of toys was something I will cherish forever.

During my junior and senior years, I took a community service course and was involved with young children. In my junior year, I volunteered at the local YMCA Early Learning Center with three and four-year olds. I was able to develop relationships with them and be a role model to them through my experience there. During my senior year, I gained 21 new little friends in a kindergarten class at St Mary's Primary School in Taunton. I saw them at least two-three days a week, so we all grew very close.

Now that I am in my first semester of college, I have been able to serve at a soup kitchen, but I am still searching for the exact type of service I want to be involved in. I hope to find a program involving children. At the soup kitchen in downtown Providence, there were already many volunteers, so my friend and I were assigned to dish washing. Although we were not able to have direct contact with the people eating, we still felt the profound feeling of service. The director of the kitchen explained to us how grateful she was that we came because her normal dishwasher didn't show up. Such a simple task of washing dishes made such a great impact on the kitchen.

My acts of service have taught me that every little bit helps. Whether organizing toys, registering names, or washing dishes, you never know how much your help can impact a community. I have learned that the people in our communities with the least can be the most grateful people in the world. I have also learned that when I serve, I should go into each situation with an open mind and an open heart. My service to others has taught me that it doesn't take much to make a change in some people's lives. Some people just need encouragement.

In the future, I hope to become involved in or even create a program with young girls that have experienced abuse themselves or within their families. In this program, the girls will be taught self-esteem, respect, and confidence in their future and their communities. Growing up, I was the oldest in my family and had two younger sisters. Our father struggled with domestic violence and alcohol abuse problems. When he abused my sisters' mother, I always explained to my sisters that this was not a normal way of living and to never let anyone belittle you or hurt you. Once my sisters moved with their mother's family and I was placed in the care of my grandparents, I felt assured that I had left my sisters with a good sense of self-esteem and a model of how a woman should be respected and treated.

Dr. Martin Luther King Jr. lived by the Bible verse stated at the beginning of my essay, and through his life he taught the world that even the least of our society deserves to live a prosperous life. He sacrificed his life time and time again to give people the chance for equality and a fair life. He advocated for peace and respect in our society. By following Dr. King's model, I have been able to help those in our community that are less fortunate and have striven to make our community a better place.

Cierra Greene
2016 3rd Place Winner

8

Helping Others to be Their Best

I do not serve others by doing volunteer work or community service, but my two jobs (Bob's Auto Repair and TJ Maxx), school, and cross country give me the chance to serve all different types of people. I help people with car problems find supplies they need around the store, help students with their homework, and help team members improve their running.

My two jobs require me to serve a variety of people in different ways every day.

When I am in school, I serve students by helping them with their homework, helping them understand a lesson topic that was taught, or just being there for them when they need someone. I really like to help students with their homework, especially if it is math. I love math. Two or three days a week after school I help a fourth grader with his math homework. Just seeing his face when he finally understands the homework, makes me feel so happy. If a student doesn't understand what we learned and I know how to apply what we learned, I try to teach it to them in a simpler way. Also, in school I help students with issues they may be having. For example, if someone isn't having a good day, I try to cheer them up. Being in school gives me a lot of opportunities to serve.

In cross country I serve by being a positive addition to the team, and helping my running mates improve their running.

Being a positive addition to the team is helpful because it gives others motivation and makes them try harder. Even when someone is having a bad day, being a positive team member can cheer them up. I also help my teammates become better runners by running with those who are a little bit slower. Finally, as a former captain it is my job to make everyone feel a part of the team and the best runner they can be!

I have learned many important lessons by serving others, but one lesson stands out to me more than most. I've learned that it is more valuable to give than receive. When I help others, it makes me feel like I have accomplished something and have done something right. Serving others also makes me feel like I have a purpose, and makes me feel like I am a better person.

In the future I want to help kids in the Foster Care system and show them that even when you are in the deepest, darkest place you can imagine, like I was, that there is always a happy ending. For the longest time I was stuck in a rut and thought there was no way out, but people helped me out of it. I know what it is like to be in Foster Care my whole life and then to be adopted, so I can relate to these kids. Even if I help one child, I will be ecstatic because I know I changed at least one person's life. Just like Martin Luther King Jr. said, "If I can help somebody as I pass along, if I can cheer somebody with a word or song, if I can show somebody he's traveling wrong, then my living will not be in vain."

Chantelle Lampert
2015 3rd Place Winner

9

Giving Is Receiving

Some people believe that life is suffering. The Buddha himself implemented this belief in the First Noble Truth. Life includes pain, aging, disease, and ultimately death. While this may be true, life isn't always suffering; as humans we try to eliminate the suffering of others everyday through our interactions with them. Whether it is modern medicine, being a good friend, or volunteering, the human race strives to help one another to reduce suffering.

Growing up I saw suffering first hand because I lived with it on a daily basis. Since I was a young child, both of my parents battled drug addiction. The Department of Children and Family Services has been active in my life for as long as I can remember and I still remain in their custody today. While my family was dealing with domestic challenges, soon after I was dealt a challenge of my own. At the age of seven, I was diagnosed with Wilms' tumor Cancer. A tumor the size of a football had grown on my left kidney. When I was eleven years old, the cancer came back, this time in the lung. I had to do it all over again; another surgery, a year and a half of chemotherapy, and this time radiation, too. I did not expect my youth to entail these complications, but it was out of my control. I had no choice but to remain strong, focused, and positive, with hope that there were brighter days ahead. In the face of these obstacles, the people in my life appeared supportive.

Looking back on it, I saw how my community, school, and friends came together to help relieve the suffering from my family and me. I am so grateful for the immense amount of support I received. Once I began remission I also made it a goal to give back to my community. I am currently involved in the Artworks! Program in New Bedford, Massachusetts. I have been involved in this teen art program for four years and it has been one of the most rewarding and enjoyable experiences of my life. Through Artworks!, my classmates and I volunteer two hours each week to better the community of New Bedford with art. Some of our contributions have included painting murals on buildings, decorating electrical boxes, and planting flowers around the city. Additionally, every week at this program I have helped younger students with their artwork. I enjoy taking part in Artworks! because it is self-rewarding to give back to my community and bring people joy in the form of art.

In addition to the community service I do at Artworks! I also take part in the Gifts to Give Program every year at Christmastime. This program wraps donated toys for children who are less fortunate and may not receive much around the holidays. I really enjoy this program because I genuinely enjoy giving back to my community and helping people who are less fortunate than I.

The most important lesson I have learned from serving others is that giving is receiving; when I give I feel a sense of wholeness. Also, another important lesson I have learned is that nothing in life is guaranteed and you never know when you may be the one suffering and in need for support. I have been in a position where I was in need of help and I am so appreciative to have received it. Now I strive to give back to my community and am inspired to help others.

How we interpret our sufferings and integrate them into our lives is fundamental to how we coexist with them. I did not expect these life obstacles as a teenager, but I knew I had to be resilient and keep excelling in school so I could have the opportunity to go to college and obtain a degree and give back. With my degree I intend to open a private art therapy practice. My dream is to work with sick children and teens and help them express their emotions through art.

Alexandra Xifaras
2015 3rd Place Winner

The Beautiful Struggle

It is easy in a society plagued with poverty and injustice to wallow in pessimism—to deny the beauty of the forest because of the ugliness of some of its trees. There seems to be never-ending war, a constant toil for peace and, for some, simply survival. And yet, in spite of this unfortunate state of the nation, there is an undying beauty in the struggle.

Altruism is defined as the unselfish concern for the welfare of others. Every day presents thousands of opportunities for acts of kindness. Sometimes it's the holding a door for someone, other times an anonymous donation to non-profit organizations, hours volunteered at the nearby homeless shelter, and many times it is the time spent with a struggling friend. As Saint Francis of Assisi said, "It is in giving that one receives."

Today, I have the tremendous pleasure of working with teenagers in early recovery from drug addiction. Ironically, I was a client in the same program three years ago. There have been countless days when I went home with a gratitude so tremendous I was brought to tears. I am ever reminded when going to work or walking around my city of where I used to be—homeless, helpless, and drug-addicted. If it weren't for the selflessness of my community, I probably wouldn't be alive today, let alone clean and sober and striving toward a college education.

And so, it is my responsibility to give freely what was given to me: to love others with a passion, to give without expectation for return, and to listen. It is my responsibility to be present and proactive in this life that can sometimes be incredibly frightening to face. As Dr. Martin Luther King once said, "We must forever conduct our struggle on the high plane of dignity and discipline."

Melinda Lee
2011 3rd Place Winner

PART THREE

They Chose to Find Purpose Through Serving

"Life's most persistent and urgent question is, 'What are you doing for others?'"[3]

11

A Drum Major for Children

My name is David Burnham. I am currently in DCF care on a voluntary agreement. I am a student at Northern Essex Community College majoring in Human Services. I am on the Dean's list and will be graduating with an Associate's degree in May 2009. My plan is to begin attending Salem State College in September, where I will be studying for my Bachelors Degree in Social Work.

The people I want to serve are children and families in the Lawrence area. My long-term goal is to become a social worker for DCF in Lawrence. I currently serve adolescents in DCF care by participating in the North East Youth Advisory Board, and I am working with the Foster Children of the Merrimack Valley Inc. to develop and establish a mentor program. My goal is to make adolescents' lives easier while in foster care. In addition to attending college, I also work at an adolescent group home as a youth counselor. Every day I work towards being a good role model and showing teens that even though they are in foster care, the world is theirs and they can be whatever they want in the future.

I feel strongly that if each of us helps others, the world will be a better place. As a child growing up in foster care, I often felt there was no one else that knew what I was feeling. I am proud that I can perhaps be the person who will let a child know they are not alone. After reading how Dr.

Martin Luther King wanted to be remembered as a drum major for justice, peace, and righteousness, I hope that someday I may be successful enough to be remembered as a drum major for children in foster care.

David Burnham
2010 3rd Place Winner

12

Love Leaves Its Mark

Volunteering is an unconditional act of love. It transcends time and leaves its mark on the people it has touched, long after the act has been done. As time passes, it grows like an eternal flame, forever burning in your heart. To be honest, I have not volunteered in a year because of the pressures of school and work, but the desire to do so is still in my heart. In school, I am currently an English major, focusing on Rhetoric and Communication with a minor in Literature. Although it has been a while, I plan on getting back into volunteering this semester. My school has many volunteering opportunities, such as the Y-Farm and the Kids to College program. They even have a whole department, the Leduc Civic Engagement Center dedicated to service.

I still find ways to stay connected with my community through my job. I work at a school, and the many ways I serve the kids allows me to give back. I am a tutor at schools in New Bedford and Fall River. At the school in New Bedford I work with kindergarten children and at the school in Fall River I work with fifth grade children. The different age groups challenge me because they expect different things from me intellectually.

I decided to work with kids because of the way that I was influenced by my mentors growing up. I remember specifically in seventh grade when one of my mentors believed in me enough to tell me that I was good enough and intelligent enough to go to college. For me, that made the difference, and pushed me even further to achieve my dreams. It made me realize that our words have power; long after they are spoken or written, they still have power in the minds of the people they have touched.

During seventh grade, I was chosen to be in a leadership camp that changed my life. Through the program I had to keep up my grades and also volunteer a specified number of hours per year, depending on my grade. It kept me focused on my education and humbled me as an individual. Volunteering became an important part of my life because of the way that it made me feel as well as the influence that I had on the people around me.

Growing up I had a difficult childhood but I never let the circumstances define my success as a person. In times that are tough, you make the decision to either let a situation consume you or overcome it by fighting back. I have met many great people in my life. The struggles that they were going through did not compare to mine; it was in that moment that I learned the importance of compassion and the value of self-worth.

In retrospect, serving others was an outlet. I was going through some trying times and the people that I volunteered with really helped me get through them. During that time I was a candy striper in a hospital near my town, and I never realized the impact it had on me until this moment. In school I was the quiet girl, the smart girl, nothing more. Working with strangers and helping them, I could just be Sherline. I was not confined by the labels that my family, classmates and friends place on me. It made me feel important and confident in my abilities as a person.

Overall, serving or helping others is important to me. Without the generous help of people who are willing to give up their time to help you, a complete stranger—some people would probably not have food to eat or even clothes on their back. Volunteerism is an important life lesson. It gives people who desperately need help a way out without losing their dignity. It has taught me that no matter what I am going through someone might have it worse. In this life, drive is important, hard work is essential, but serving and having the ability to give is crucial. Not everyone is dealt the same hand and, without the help of others, life would be intolerable. We all need help sometimes no matter how hard it is to receive it, especially when we might feel like we are less than deserving.

The act of service does not see the color of your skin, your appearance, or your status. It does not judge you on your merit or your good works. You are regarded purely for the intentions behind your service. It is an act of love disguised by the label of service. In serving others you find purpose and strength within yourself to overcome obstacles and become a better person.

Sherline Dorcelus
2014 3rd Place Winner

13

To be Great, is to be Giving

My name is Brooke Munafo. I know that I want to be great, important, and significant. This is my "Drum Major Instinct." However, it is not all about me; it is about my life and what I accomplish. It is about my daily interactions with people, the promises that I make to others, my helping hands, and giving the best I can give to anyone in any way throughout my life. This is how I achieve and harness the "Drum Major Instinct" that Martin Luther King described. It is my instinct to serve others.

Why do I want to help others? Have you ever needed help? After I first realized that I needed help, it prompted me to make the decision to help and serve others that are in need. As a child, I was deprived of childhood fun and happiness. This made for a depressing life. Although this feeling was burdensome, I knew it would not last forever. I promised myself that I would strive for a better life. Nobody should feel this way—depressed, lonely, and deprived of the necessities of life. The pain was hurtful to the heart. Understanding that some individuals do not have the strength I had to believe that Life is better than what it may seem at the moment, I vowed to serve and help them through difficulties. I am now grateful that God put me through this to test me and make me stronger. God was next to me growing up and I knew I was not alone in my pain. Understanding my need for help, I knew that I wanted to teach other people that they are strong too and can overcome their pain.

I have been in many situations in which I served both people and animals. For one week, two years in a row, I went to Juarez Mexico to build shelters and feed homeless children. I have attended multiple charity walks raising money, volunteered at soup kitchens, and helped at animal shelters. I am always there to help family and friends. It is evident I do not need to be asked twice; I will go anywhere to help anyone or anything.

Currently I am attending school at Bryant University. One reason I chose this school is because it has outstanding community outreach programs. On campus I am involved in Big Brothers Big Sisters. I have a little sister whom I meet every Monday afternoon. There are multiple events that Big Sisters host on and off campus to serve, such as: helping out at soup kitchens, raising money for breast cancer, and writing letters for Saint Jude's Hospital. This past October I took a leadership position to have the Sisters raise money and participate in the Walk for Breast Cancer. In the future, I hope to run for and hold the position of president in Big Sisters. As president, I would like to expand our service all around the state in order to have more Big Brothers and Sisters to serve more children. I want to give as much as possible. Martin Luther King has proved and stated that to be great, is to be giving.

Brooke Munafo
2012 3rd Place Winner

PART FOUR

They Chose to Give Back

"The time is always right to do what is right."[4]

14

Helping Others Enriches the Giver

Dr. Martin Luther King, Jr. lived his life to serve others and stand up for human rights. Although serving may be beneficial to the people we help, I can personally say that helping people has brought meaning, self worth, and happiness to my life, as well as guidance to stay on the right path. Knowing you gave someone hope and the feeling that they matter, is one of the greatest things you can ever experience.

My first venture into serving started with the Dracut Skate Park where I have worked as a monitor for about 5 years. The Town of Dracut does not want the kids skating at local businesses or public parks, so a skate park was built to give kids a place to go. When I first started, kids had to fill out forms and pay to use the park. Growing up, our family didn't have a lot of money, and this held me back from doing a lot of the things I wanted to do. When I would talk to kids about having to pay, I saw the same face that I used to make when I would be turned down because of money. This really hit home so I started to work with the Town Recreation Department to get rid of those requirements.

The park is open only seasonally from Memorial Day to the end of October and only from 3 p.m. to 7 p.m. As a skater for ten years, I know that the kids want to skate more than that. So, I plan to try to get rid of these limited time frames. I plan on being the voice for the skaters when I am at town meetings, and I plan on being the voice for the town when I meet with the kids who use the park. I told my boss that it would mean more to me to not have a job as skateboarding manager, which is the best job I ever had, if it meant the kids could use the skate park at any time of the day. It has also been a rewarding experience knowing that I have helped show the town that these kids are not troublemakers, which seems to be the misconception about skaters.

My services with the skate park do not end there. I would have to turn kids down if they didn't have a helmet; they didn't have one because the kids' parents did not want to "waste money" on a helmet. When I asked the Rec Department if they could supply helmets, they were unsuccessful. I then took it upon myself to gather helmets from friends and strangers. By doing this, I noticed a dramatic increase in the number of kids who showed up at the park.

But the kids never had a drink or money to get one—and the park does not even have a water bubbler! I knew what it was like to skate all day with no water, no food, and no money, so I took it upon myself to bring down gallons of water every day. I also bought cheeseburgers from Wendy's and bags of chips for the kids. Although I like to make sure their stomachs are full and they are not dehydrated, I like to make them do a little work, too. If the kids want some water or something to eat, I have them pick up trash around the park. I'm really proud to say that I have helped the kids become better skateboarders and better people.

A remarkable thing happened: the kids started serving each other by teaching each other tricks. The whole skate park would get involved when someone was trying something new, which I have never seen anywhere else. The Dracut Skate Park has become a community and we all help each other.

My college experience hasn't been ideal. I have lived in eight different places, including a tent, since I started college. I felt lost trying to find my way through the school, logging on to computers, filling out the correct paperwork, and going to the right offices and buildings. I know I am not the only one who has dealt with this. I attended a foster care awareness event at UMass Lowell last year and I met a student and teacher who were interested in starting a club to help foster kids and homeless kids. I was instantly drawn in, and during fall semester we started having meetings, founding the Navigators Club. There were many discussions about whom we would help and what we would do. During these discussions I felt it was important to help not only foster kids and homeless students but also to help anyone who may feel lost. I have high hopes and big plans for this club! I have talked to so many students who aren't foster kids who love this idea and feel that they would benefit from it. It feels so good to know that I am a founding member of this club and to know that this club has the potential to help so many students.

I love to help people and know I impact someone's life in a positive way. My life hasn't been easy but the handful of people who have been there for me have really made the difference in how I handle my situations. Now that I've gotten a taste of what it is like to serve, I have been dedicating a lot of time to it.

I am currently trying to get involved with CASA (Court Appointed Special Advocates) because this program hits home for me and I want to be there for a child who is going through the worst times of his/her life.

A quote from Martin Luther King, Jr. best describes the way I feel about serving others: "If I can help somebody as

I pass along, if I can cheer somebody with a word or song, if I can show somebody he's traveling wrong, then my living will not be in vain."

David Daigle
2012 1st Place Winner

15

Standing Up for Others

As a child in the foster care system, I was often in search of help. The best person available was my social worker. For that reason, I have decided that I want to become a social worker, too, so I can help serve youth in need.

I do not live with either of my parents and there are many things in my everyday life that I need an adult for. My social worker has always been there for me. For example, when I had to quickly get my passport, she was a great resource, and I don't know what I would have done if she hadn't helped me make my school trip to England and France—a trip that had a huge impact on my life. It was the first time I ever got on a plane and I was able to use my academic knowledge on the journey overseas. As a social worker, I would work tirelessly to help all the foster children who need an understanding adult in their lives.

Currently, I serve the elderly community by volunteering at a Haitian day and health center. I have been doing that for the past three years. In addition, I have served young people by volunteering at Cradles to Crayons, preparing backpacks for children to go to school. Also, I spent the summer of 2012 serving the developmentally disabled people in my community through a job opportunity known as the Urban Youth collaborative. When I signed up for this, it wasn't the money that motivated me but rather being exposed to a different sector of the community that is often ostracized. I learned a lot about myself and my capacity for love. After this experience, I began feeling differently about those who are labeled "retarded." I encourage my family and friends not to use this word. After two months the program ended, but I decided to stay on so I would not be just another face that they got used to and never saw again.

Throughout my life, so many people have been there for me, but about 90 % of them are no longer involved with me. In some cases, it makes me feel bad and in others it makes me wonder why they didn't stay in my life. I want to be the person who sticks around for those in need, whether it is youth or the elderly.

I was taken away from my mother at age six, and from then on my life became a rollercoaster. Bouncing from house to house after being in a foster home and getting adopted, I went through a great deal of heartache in my life. Just as I have always had a few people in my hard knock life that gave me a helping hand, I believe it is only right for me to do the same for others.

Givona J. Dietz
2013 3rd Place Winner

16

Shaped by My Past

Martin Luther King, Jr. was a revolutionary man. He spoke of non-violent ways to create a society of equality that stirred many people's hearts. My dreams and hopes of everyday life are motivated by the inspirational quote, "I have a dream that one day this nation will rise up and live out the true meaning of its creed: we hold these truths to be self-evident, that all men are created equal." Since I was a young girl, I always dreamed of a world where people could live in a free place—no fighting, no hunger, no death, no worrying about education. All this makes me never forget where I came from

The expression, "Never forget where you come from," might mean to never forget one's roots and families, but for me it also has a literal meaning. I will never forget the country I came from, or the people and events that have helped me become the strong person I am today. I was born in the central African country called the Democratic Republic of Congo. I remember eight years of a normal life. I have happy memories of my country before war broke out, but the memories that have affected me the most are from events that happened during and after the war. I have seen violence, the realities of hunger, and the effects of fear. When I hear people say, "Never forget where you come from," I know I will never forget because the people of my childhood, my family, and my birth country have all affected me and shaped me.

Growing up wasn't easy as a refugee. The good that came from so much moving is that I speak five languages—Kinyarwanda, Luganda, English, Swahili and French. The negative part is that I saw many things. I witnessed people killing each other; I saw the fear of death in peoples' eyes and sensed the hopelessness in peoples' hearts. I was only a child, but I felt very mature. Being a refugee was always very difficult. I couldn't go to school for two years because the school wasn't free and my parents couldn't afford to pay for it. In 2011, our family was told that we were moving to America.

My first day in the United States was probably the happiest day of my life. I couldn't stop imagining my life in this land of freedom and opportunity. Finally, I could stop worrying about my education, my family's safety, and our lack of freedom. I felt for the first time that I could control the outcome of my life. I finally knew that my dream of studying international relations and being able to help others was a possibility. I want to help less fortunate people like I was helped.

I have been able to give back to my community by volunteering. Every year I have helped out at the Lowell Folk Festival, I organized books at the library, and I have also been volunteering at the International Institute for three years as a youth leader. At the Institute, I have been able to communicate with different kinds of people, translate for new refugee arrivals, and tutor newly arrived refugee students who barely speak English.

As I graduate from high school this year, and reflect on the long ourney I have taken to get here, I can't wait to go to college and see my dreams come true. I believe in helping others as Martin Luther King, Jr. did. One day, I hope to impact the world through service—maybe I will work with the United Nations to give back to the community and the world.

Rehema Rwakabuba
2015 3rd Place Winner

Finding Purpose

The instrumentals of Daddy's little girl plays in the background, mixed with the laughter of children, six to ten years of age, running around the playground playing tag. It is a bright sunny day. The fragrance of flowers fully bloomed and the sweet yet savory appetizing aroma of hot dogs and caramelized coconuts being grilled fills the air. A seven-year-old little girl in a white dress runs to the swings, revealing dimples the size craters. She sits and watches the clear blue sky as her mother gently pushes her. It's beautiful, the little girl thinks, feeling so amazed. Higher and higher she goes on the swing. Then suddenly, the sun flares at her now squinting eyes and blurred vision. The rusted chain she was holding onto disappears. The seat that tightly hugged her bottom is gone. It's blinding white. Too young to understand what is going on, she sits there, falling endlessly into the vortex of reality as the bright light is interrupted by splashes of red blood.

The blood of her mother as her father strikes her with an iron pipe, smashing all her teeth. It's the blood of her mother as her father beats her up at night in the middle of the street, breaking her arm and bruising her lips. It's the blood of an eleven-year-old little girl as her drunken father stomped on her head to shut up her little sobs when she wept on the cold hard floor of the rundown apartment. Useless. Good for nothing. Waste of rice. Disappointment.

A sharp pain bolts from her rear up to her neck as she finally hits the ground. The sky is black and white. A colorful stranger lends her a helping hand, lifting her up off the ground, smiles, and walks away. She clenches her hands together, puts them to her chest, and looks around. Her mother is nowhere to be found. Disoriented, she walks back home only to discover that nobody is there. Sitting outside on the curb of the sidewalk, a puddle of water betrays her, revealing her bloodshot and raccoon-like eyes, as well as the scar between her right temple and hairline.

Her once childlike features are mutated into that of a fifteen-year-old. The white dress she was wearing is now stained with the color red and soiled with dirt. The colorful stranger walks by and asks her if she was hurt. Help me, she whispered. Without hesitation, the colorful stranger lends his hands many times more. Her white dress, once stained with red and dirt, is now filled with orange, yellow, and green. Smiles and laughter dominate her future, even though blood and trauma dictate her past.

Life is weird. I often wonder what in the world I am here for. Then I recall the reason why, and smile. I might not know what my purpose is, but I do know one thing—if I am here, I might as well make the best of it. Anything will seem depressing if you have a negative attitude and that's why I'm going to look on the bright side: count all the little things that make life great.

She smiles, looking up at the beautiful fluorescent sky, breathes in the nostalgic scent of hotdogs and coconuts. Then she looks down at the puddle of water to see that her mother has been with her all this time. Her mother lives in her in the form of the girl's petite ears, wide eyes, narrow lips, fragile smile, and strong chin.

Life has thrown rocks at her, giving her cuts and bruises, leaving a scar to serve as a constant reminder that the past was real. Made wise by unimaginable terrors, this young girl is now seventeen years old. Although branded a dog and a fly's favorite meal, she maintains a positive attitude and is focused on her main goal in life, which is helping others. What else can I do? She asks herself. Life is full of despicable, heart-wrenching evil, smothered with violence and hatred. But, life is also full of remarkable generosity, overflowing with love and laughter. I don't know the true meaning of life but I have found a purpose. Serving others, doing good deeds for the community, making a difference, spreading love, motivating and inspiring others to do well, is my reason for living. Life is hard, but made easier with compassion.

This young girl has blossomed into a young lady sovereign by hope. She stands with her ATASK family, holding one sign that says STOP RAPE, and the other, LOVE DOES NOT EQUAL ABUSE. She educates others with hopes of enlightening them. She donates her time to charitable organizations that give food to the needy, such as the Bread of Life and Walk for Hunger. At a non-profit organization called MAP, she facilitates workshops and brainstorms lessons on safe sex to prevent the spread of HIV and STDs. In her spare time, she helps out her community by tutoring or cleaning. Her dream is to open up a multilingual shelter for persons in abusive relationships dedicated to her endearing mother. This same girl is the person I see in the mirror as I brush my teeth in the morning, smiling, wondering what difference I may make that day.

Evy Tran
2011 1st Place Winner

18

Paying It Forward

I entered the foster care system when I was eleven. Since then I have lived nine years in what I consider the best part of my life. When I was first placed in a foster home I was a rebellious and sassy child. I felt that I knew everything, and since I had been hurt so badly I wasn't willing to let people help me. I was all about looking out for myself and I didn't truly care about others. However, after about two years of living with the same foster family, I began to change; I began to grow into the person I am today. I went from a girl who had a drive but no real direction, to a young woman with a full scholarship pursuing her goals at the college of her dreams.

Though at one point I was a very self-centered person, I am now a person who gives my all to whatever I can for those who need me. I learned that in life you must give in order to receive. But I also found that the best things are given with no hopes of receiving something in return. Since I have been helped to come so far in my life, I try to help those who are in the position I was in only a few years ago.

I am still living with the foster parents I was placed with eight years ago, and my foster mom still takes in teenage girls. Most of these young girls come to the house the same way I did. They have attitudes and make flip remarks. They refuse to listen to anybody. But as much as they try to act like they don't care, I have learned that they really do. A lot of the girls come to the house and they tell me how they aren't doing well in school, and that it doesn't matter. They don't bother to try to get good grades, and they don't involve themselves. I know where they are coming from. I've been there. And I talk to them about it. Since I'm only a few years older than a lot of these girls, they are able to connect with me. I found that they have an easier time talking to a peer more than an adult authority figure. I try and connect with each girl in some way. I listen to them, I talk to them, and I give them advice when it's needed. I tell them that good grades and joining in do matter in life, and if they apply themselves they have a shot at doing something amazing with their lives. Some of them listen, they all agree, but not all of them actually do something. The ones that do, get involved in sports, or choir, or the art club. They put the effort into getting better grades so that they can go to college. Recently, I had a girl tell me that she never knew what an impact grades could make on her life. Until she came to my house, she had considered school no big deal. I can proudly say that she made the honor roll this past semester, and that she is making friends, and she is working on creating a good life for herself.

My goal in life is to help as many people as I can. I want to "pay it forward" and make a difference in others' lives. Right now, it's the foster girls that come into my house, but in the future, I plan to open my own theatre where children can learn to express themselves and become confident in who they are. As Martin Luther King said, "Everybody can be great because everybody can serve." My goal in life is to serve as many people as I can, and make a difference.

Jessica Corsentino
2010 2nd Place Winner

PART FIVE

They Chose to Become Leaders by Standing up for Others

"Injustice anywhere is a threat to justice everywhere."[6]

19

Dedicated to Making a Difference

"You don't have to have a college degree to serve. You don't have to make your subject and your verb agree to serve. You don't have to know about Plato and Aristotle to serve. You don't have to know Einstein's theory of relativity to serve... you only need a heart full of grace. A soul generated by love. And you can be that servant."

— MLK, Jr.

Inspired by Dr. King and Jesus Christ, I have devoted my life to serving others. Even if I am not able to "change the world," I have learned that it is possible to make a difference. For me, a life without making a difference is not a valuable or notable one – I want to be remembered on earth for what I did to serve others.

In the past, I have helped and served others in a myriad of ways. One of my proudest accomplishments within the community was organizing the 1st Annual Shawn Fights Cancer 5K Run/Walk at Szot Park in Chicopee. The walk took place in May 2010 and was organized for a student who played on my school's football team—and whom I had never met. It was sophomore year, and I learned that my schoolmate, Shawn Cruzado, had been diagnosed with Stage 2 Testicular Cancer. For six months, I dedicated my life to raising funds to assist his family with medical expenses – $20,000 was raised.

The following year I became the chairperson for the Relay for Life of Greater Holyoke and Chicopee. The Relay for Life brought together hundreds of people and dozens of teams, whom I helped recruit, for an overnight event that raises over $85,000 annually to put an end to cancer. Cancer never sleeps, and at Relay For Life, neither do we.

Most recently, I have served people around me, coordinating volunteers and managing the office for Mayor Alex Morse of Holyoke's reelection campaign. My day-to-day responsibilities in this role consisted of directing volunteers, overseeing expenditures and areas of the budget, and most importantly knocking on doors to register voters and get our campaign message out. Face to face interaction with residents is the most rewarding component of a campaign, and is a service in itself. I have empowered neighbors near and far around the City of Holyoke to use their voice through civic engagement and in their local government to help bring changes that will benefit us all.

At the present time, I am practicing a life committed to serving others by establishing a food pantry at Holyoke Community College called the CommUNITY Cupboard. The most important part about this food pantry is that it serves the school's population, the students themselves. It is not right or fair for anyone to face hunger, and it is particularly difficult and distracting to face hunger while pursuing an education.

In the future, I dream of helping and serving others in more than one way. Whether it be the small gesture of giving someone a ride to their polling location on Election Day to vote, inviting someone in need over to share dinner with me on Thanksgiving Day, or something as large as developing an organization to provide an outlet for struggling youth, I plan to make a difference.

As Martin Luther King, Jr. once said, "I just want to leave a committed life behind...If I can help somebody as I pass along, if I can cheer somebody with a word or song, if I can show somebody he's traveling wrong, then my living will not be in vain..."

Elvin Bruno
2014 2nd Place Winner

Fighting for Justice

Martin Luther King Jr. led a life of service and because of his sacrifice millions of people have been positively impacted. In his speech he says he wants his life to be remembered for his work, to inspire, to guide and to bring happiness to people. I am confident that his life was not in vain but had the impact he wished. His life has provided the inspiration and empowerment many have needed in a battle that has yet to be won. His role as a civil rights leader, humanitarian, and social issues activist is so important to our community. Dr. King was a substantial force to be reckoned with. If I can make just a quarter of the impact he has made I will be pleased.

"Injustice anywhere is a threat to justice everywhere." This quote from Dr. King constantly plays in my head and makes me fight for any and every injustice I see because to know of such and not speak means I am just as guilty. Like Dr. King I see myself as a servant, a servant to those who may need an advocate, a crutch or simply a voice. I do not help, advocate, or seek change for recognition; I do it because it is the right thing to do and I would want someone to do it for me.

In today's society along with the racial issues that continue to haunt us, we also have other issues adding to the tribulation: homelessness, unequal playing fields, unlivable wages, mass incarceration, police brutality, and increasing rents. As one can see, there is plenty of work to be done. Life has chosen me to tackle homelessness and unequal playing fields for men of color.

In 2012, my family and I became homeless. Due to this misfortune, my goal of becoming a social worker at DCF shifted to another population that I believe urgently needed my attention. As my family and I sought assistance an unjust system appeared before us. Families with two parent households were being targeted and men were being separated from their families. After suffering such a tragic experience my calling became even clearer.

I used this adversity to fuel my drive to advocate for the homeless population: primarily, to denounce the separation of families and, then, to assist the men the system had plucked and thrown to the side. Because I am a firm believer that a home, food, and bare necessities are not luxuries but human rights, I could not stay quiet. This experience started out negatively but has had many positive outcomes. In April 2014, I gave a speech at the Homes for Families legislative breakfast about the effects of homelessness and the negative impact the separation of my family had. Congressman Mike Capuano and Senator Chang-Diaz, were present. I was told after my speech that bringing light to the separation of families has caused DHCD to implement new policies to combat these unacceptable practices, allowing more men into shelter. In October 2015, I incorporated my very own nonprofit, Vi's House for Hope, which distributes a hot meal, care packages, and winter necessities at least once a month to homeless people sleeping on the streets in and around Boston.

I continue to stand with Homes for Families to advocate for more funding for affordable permanent housing. The next upcoming event is Cookie Day, February 4, 2016, at the Massachusetts State House from 10 am to noon. VI's House for Hope's next community outreach is January 21, 2016. One day, my nonprofit will be a community resource center and a long-term sober men's shelter.

Although I have made progress, I know there is still plenty to be done and I am committed to fighting for people for as long as it may take. On my journey, I will continue to hear and use Dr. King's quote, "Injustice anywhere is a threat to justice everywhere. We are caught in an inescapable network of mutuality, tied in a single garment of destiny. Whatever affects one directly, affects all indirectly."

Judith Frey
2016 3rd Place Winner

21

Giving Back Every Day

Dr. Martin Luther King once said, "Everybody can be great because everybody can serve." Serving others allows all individuals, whether black or white, rich or poor, to feel a sense of greatness and accomplishment. I have served others who were less fortunate since I was a young girl. My first experience with serving was during the seventh grade as a volunteer at a local food pantry. Since then, my experiences with serving the community have lead me to want to pursue a career in teaching, a career that will allow me to give back every day.

During the summer of 2010, I was able to serve others indirectly. I worked with a coworker to create Work It Off!, an application for the Android phone. The application is aimed at adolescents and teaches individuals the correlation between caloric intake and exercise. My coworker and I submitted Work It Off! to Michelle Obama's Apps for Healthy Kids contest as part of the First Lady's Let's Move campaign to help fight child obesity. Work It Off! was honored in September 2010 at the White House and has been distributed via the web for individuals to use on their Android phones.

In the fall of 2010 I began serving others directly, by working with a neighborhood technology center that is sponsored by Trinity College. The center, known as Trinfo.Cafe, provides free computer and internet access to the residents of Hartford, CT. In addition, free computer literacy classes are offered for patrons as well as after school programs for students. The center was created to help decrease the digital divide between the poverty stricken city and the wealthy, private college that lies in the middle of it. All of the services at Trinfo.Cafe are provided by Trinity College students such as myself. I began my work at Trinfo.Cafe as a volunteer who taught a self-designed after school program on how to create applications for Android phones. I offered the class to local high school students, free of charge. During the summer of 2011 I was hired as a paid employee at the center to help manage the facility. However, I still wanted to serve by volunteering and teaching the course I had designed. Since the fall of 2010, I have run and taught the after school program three times. Each time I find that teaching the students is very rewarding because I am able to share my knowledge with them and they help me to better myself both as a person and as a teacher, an experience that can't be bought.

Currently I am a junior at Trinity College and I am majoring in both Computer Science and Educational Studies. My career goal is to become a high school computer Science/Technology teacher. I wish to take the skills that I have learned from Trinfo.Cafe and apply them to my future career as a teacher. I have not decided where I would like to live after college, but I know that no matter where I end up I can always give back to the community by sharing my knowledge and skills with others who are less fortunate than I. I have also considered starting a center similar to Trinfo.Cafe in the location that I move to.

Pauline Lake
2012 2nd Place Winner

22

Serving from the Heart

Dr. King said the root of being great is serving: "You only need a heart full of grace. A soul generated by love. And you can be that servant." I have gained this heart and soul through my experiences as a foster child, serving on many community initiatives as a volunteer, and through interning at a foster care agency.

I was only thirteen years old when I entered the foster care system; that was nine years ago. Since then I have been in many foster and group homes and have had many difficult, as well as healing, experiences. It is only now as a twenty-two- year-old, that I am able to reflect on those experiences and realize how formative they were in creating the person I am today. As a child from my background and history, I have experienced first-hand how important it is to have at least one positive influence. I was blessed to have a few. These women, like angels, took me under their wings and helped create what Dr. King referred to as my "heart full of grace and my soul generated by love." These individuals lived a life that radiated love and compassion for others and captured my heart and guided me on a path of love and giving.

Through these individuals' strong dedication to others and to me, I was taught the value of sharing my love with those who were in need. I became a "Big" for Big Brothers/Big Sisters and spent many afternoons at Therapeutic

Equestrian centers. I wanted to offer my love and support to other children, just as my angels had done for me. In both these volunteer opportunities, it was so heartwarming to see how much of a positive influence each volunteer and I had on the children we were sharing our love and time with.

In addition to volunteering for Big Brothers/Big Sisters and Therapeutic Equestrian centers, I also joined a few groups that were looking out for the youth who still were in foster care. I spent time on the boards of the DCF Youth Advisory, H.E.R.O.E.S. program, and the Foster Youth Alumni of Massachusetts. I wanted to be part of groups that had the potential to help change the experiences for children living within the foster care system. The volunteers on these three boards, as well as all the volunteers for Big Brothers/Big Sisters and the Therapeutic Equestrian centers, radiated hearts guided by grace and souls filled with love for the children they were serving. This was obvious through their dedication to help these children without any financial compensation.

I just finished a semester-long internship with teenage foster youth. I was once one of them, so this particular population was very near and dear to my heart. It was eye-opening to see that the struggles I experienced as a thirteen-year-old were the same struggles these thirteen-year-olds, almost ten years later, were experiencing. They were in and out of group homes and lock-ups for doing petty, and sometimes serious, crimes. They were roaming the streets and doing drugs. They were skipping class and mouthing-off to authority figures. I wondered, how could all the same struggles persist? Why wasn't it better? After all, this was a new generation. Shouldn't life outcomes have improved for this generation? Then it came to me. There was a very basic human need missing for many of these foster youth. Many of these children were lacking love.

Many of us take for granted the human need for feeling loved. The people who are lucky enough to be loved unconditionally do not always understand that some humans have never felt this very important and necessary part of being human. The struggles in this population were clearly rooted in the youth not feeling loved, and, in turn, seeking it in all the wrong places or trying to prove they were not loveable by doing hurtful things to others. They had not been exposed to adults who had hearts guided by grace and souls generated by love that Dr. King stressed was so important for us to be "great." These youth would now be labeled as "troubled," the opposite of "great," because they were not able to experience the value of those two parts of us that Dr. King spoke of.

Now that I have finished the internship with the teenage foster youth, I will be doing an internship with kids from birth to five years old in foster care this coming spring semester. This will be my final semester of my Bachelor's degree and I have applied to go on for my Master's in social work this coming fall. I hope to one day open up a nonprofit organization that offers animal therapy to foster youth. If there's one thing I have learned throughout my life experiences, volunteering, and interning, it's that if we want to help a child thrive, we must show them the goodness of a heart full of grace and a soul generated by love.

Skye Schiller
2015 2nd Place Winner

23

Maximum Impact

Service is a word widely used but not widely acted upon. With an equally broad meaning, it may be difficult to determine the exact definition of what service is. If you ask ten different people, you will get ten different answers; and that's the beauty of it. There's no need to have one set definition of what service is, because it can mean something different for everyone. To me, service is the act of helping others through projects and ideas in order to build a stronger community.

The words of Martin Luther King, Jr. were said with boldness and the integrity to guide others. It does not take much to serve, except one's time; time that is filled with enrichment and kindness. If you are helping someone and expecting something in return, you're doing business, not kindness. Expecting something in return defeats the purpose of service; to serve is to help others without these expectations. We should be grateful if what we receive in return is knowledge.

During my first year in college, I had the pleasure to be a part of the Community Service Residential Learning Community (RLC). Within this RLC, we built a community of students passionate about service, built on the foundation of helping others. We did many service projects such as creating holiday cards for soldiers, making bagged lunches for the shelter, and spending the day with children from Big Sister Big Brother. We all joined in on the MLK day of service and helped clean a Women's shelter in Middleboro. During this time, I took it upon myself to branch out and do some service of my own. I found a cause that I was passionate about and started making phone calls. I was able to secure an interview at A New Day, a rape crisis center in Brockton, for a training to become a rape crisis counselor. After 35 hours of training I received my certificate and started volunteering immediately. My second semester as a freshman, I volunteered over 350 hours as a rape crisis counselor.

Sophomore year I was accepted into the Social Justice RLC, with many of my friends from freshman year. This RLC was focused on a specific social justice issue tailored to each student's interest. I stuck with the theme of sexual assault. A fellow student and I chose the same topic, so we worked together and were able to raise awareness and created a program that taught self-defense for any students interested. I was also honored to be a part of the Presidential Task Force on Sexual Assault Prevention. This allowed me and other like-minded people to share thoughts and ideas on how we can make our campus safer and change the stigma of sexual assault. After the task force ended, I decided to further our efforts by creating a student organization specifically made to be a place to further discuss and educate others.

As I finish up my junior year of college, I have the next semester to reflect on this past semester—from working at the Community Service Center and volunteering at homeless shelters, to my recent service trip to Cape Verde. I was grateful to have been able to spend two weeks in Cape Verde with other foster children like myself. We were able to experience the poverty and hardship of those who live there, while trying to bring hope and service to improve their communities. Meeting a spectrum of different characters; from the children of Safende, one of the poorest neighborhoods in Santiago, to meeting with the elderly and seeing how drastically different things are. This proves MLK's idea of how anyone can serve, regardless of background and in this case regardless of the language spoken. I can only hope that through my service, I have made a difference in at least one person's life while I was there, because I know that they made a difference in mine.

In the future, I hope to help people similar to who I am and who I was. My passion for helping others is my drive to become a better person every day, through my actions and my words. I strongly believe that those who do the most for others are the happiest. And through helping others, we can let them know that they are not alone; that's what is truly important. I am unsure what my future will hold, but I am certain that it will involve an undying passion to make the world a better place, not only for me, but for future generations; so they may never have to see to the issues that plague our society.

Ironically, as I sit writing this, I am wearing my MLK day of service shirt from my freshman year of college. Community service has always been a part of my life; from when I was younger and always wanting to help others, to when I became older and made that want a reality. For me, service is much more than helping others. Volunteering has given me the opportunity to learn not only about others, but about myself as well. While doing a service project, I am immersed in the people around me; listening to their stories and experiences. I am on their level, and just for a few moments, I am them. I embody what they have said, the insight that they have given; and use that as fuel for a much bigger fight. For those few hours, it is no longer about me and what I need, but about what others need. Through learning from others, I am able to learn more about myself. Who I am and what I want to be becomes clearer; rather than a blurred vision in the distance. It is with this that I realize that service is not only about helping others, but rather helping build a sense of hope in a community where hope is lacking. Just one second of hope can inspire a lifetime of change.

Taylor M. Roberts
2016 1st Place Winner

PART SIX

Next Steps in Living a Life of Significance

Cierra Greene

Givona Dietz

Pauline Lake

Amber Biswa

Bahati Mwezi

Sherline Dorcelus

24

The Journey Continues

Amber Biswa

Amber Biswa is currently attending Middlesex Community College and helps other ESL students with Math and English homework. He continues to work 25 hours a week at Shaw's Supermarket in Ashland MA, working as a cashier, bagging, training new employees, customer service and as front end manager. In the community, Amber is a drummer for a Napali church in Shrewsbury and helps newly arrived parishioners who need help in adjusting to their new culture.

Givona Dietz

Givona Dietz is currently a senior at Wheelock College studying for a Bachelor's degree in Social Work. After her graduation in the spring of 2017, she plans to attend graduate school with the goal of earning a Master's in the same field.

Givona continues to volunteer on campus, and in the community with organizations that she has been a part of growing up. She volunteers at DCF (Department of Children and Families) and Bigger Than My Block, and is currently employed as a clinical intern counseling students with Individual Educational Plans.

Sherline Dorcelus

Sherline Dorcelus recently graduated from UMASS Dartmouth with a B.A. in English, majoring in writing rhetoric and communication with a minor in literature. She is currently working in her field and hopes to earn her M.F.A. soon. She has always been passionate about literacy and education and has continued to take an active role in volunteerism through education offered through her school.

Judith Frey

Judith Frey is a senior at UMASS Boston and will be graduating in May 2017 with two bachelors' degrees, one in human services and one in sociology. She is a campus intern with UACCESS, helping students who face struggles such as homelessness, hunger, and abuse. Judith plans on attending graduate school.

Cierra Greene

Cierra Greene is currently a sophomore at the University of Rhode Island in the College of Business and just completed her first internship with Pricewaterhouse Coopers. She plans to continue her studies on the Master's level in order to become a Certified Public Accountant. Cierra continues to serve her community through volunteering with Cradles to Crayons and participating in events for PINK, an organization on campus that promotes Breast Cancer awareness and honors survivors.

Pauline Lake

Since writing her essay, Pauline Lake has earned a Bachelor's Degree from Trinity College where she studied Computer Science and Educational Studies. After graduation, Pauline began working as the teaching consultant for the Mobile Computer Science Principles Project at Trinity College.

Since 2013, the project has trained over 300 teachers and reached over 5,000 students.

Giving back through teaching and education remains a passion for Pauline, who currently teaches the intro-level Computing with Mobile Phones course at Trinity College as well as teaching mathematics for the Hartford Youth Scholars Foundation, which provides academic enrichment and high school preparation for Hartford's underserved youth. Pauline is currently pursuing a Master's Degree in Public Policy and is a proud supporter of President Obama's "CS for All" initiative. "Don't just play on your phone, program it." –President Barack Obama

Chantelle Lampert

Chantelle Lampert is currently a sophomore at UMASS Dartmouth, studying Mechanical Engineering. She would like to work with cars and robots, and she is currently a member of the Rugby Team and the school dance club.

Brooke Munafo

Brooke Munafo received her undergraduate degree in accounting from Bryant University in May 2015, and is pursuing a Masters in Taxation at Bentley University. She is currently an associate a mid-sized accounting firm located in Boston.

Brooke says, "One thing I have learned through my journey so far in life, is that access to obtain knowledge is important for development. I realized at a young age that education was my way to grow and get out of a difficult life. In the long run, education opened doors of opportunities for me. I am forever grateful for the scholarships that you and others have given me to help open these doors; they have allowed me to develop into a strong, independent, and educated woman with a life full of opportunities."

Bahati Mwezi

Bahati Mwezi is currently a senior at UMASS Amherst studying molecular biology. He has been a teaching assistant while attending UMASS and is interested in teaching as a career.

End Notes

1. Martin Luther King Jr., "Drum Major Instinct" sermon Ebenezer Baptist Church, Atlanta, GA, February 4, 1968
2. Martin Luther King Jr., A Testament of HOPE: The Essential Writings and Speeches.
3. Quote from a sermon titled "Three Dimensions of a Complete Life" by Martin Luther King Jr. 1963 Collection "Strength to Love."
4. Quote from "The Future of Integration" address at Oberlin College, October 22, 1964.
5. Quote from "Letter from a Birmingham Jail" by Dr. Martin Luther King, Jr. April 16, 1963.